Joke Books

by Judy A. Winter

Consulting Editor: Gail Saunders-Smith, PhD

CAPSTONE PRESS
a capstone imprint

Pebble Books are published by Capstone Press,
151 Good Counsel Drive, P.O. Box 669, Mankato, Minnesota 56002.
www.capstonepub.com

Books published by Capstone Press are manufactured with paper
containing at least 10 percent post-consumer waste.

Library of Congress Cataloging-in-Publication Data
Winter, Judy A., 1952–
  Jokes about monsters / by Judy A. Winter.
    p. cm. — (Pebble books. Joke books)
  Includes bibliographical references.
  Summary: "Simple text and photographs present jokes about monsters"—
Provided by publisher.
  ISBN 978-1-4296-4998-8 (library binding)
  1. Monsters—Juvenile humor. I. Title. II. Series.
PN6231.M665W56 2011
818'.602—dc22   2010002325

Editorial Credits
Gillia Olson, editor; Ted Williams, designer; Sarah Schuette, studio specialist;
    Marcy Morin, studio scheduler

Photo Credits
All photos by Capstone Studio: Karon Dubke except: Shutterstock: Guido Vrola, 6
(moon background), Igrik, cover (pearl necklace), 22, MisterElements, 4 (red devil),
trucic, throughout (background)

Note to Parents and Teachers

The Pebble Jokes set supports English language arts standards related
to reading a wide range of print for personal fulfillment. Early readers
may need assistance to read some of the words and to use the Table of
Contents, Read More, and Internet Sites sections of this book.

Printed in the United States of America in North Mankato, Minnesota.
122010   006028R

Table of Contents

Why are monsters covered with wrinkles?

Have you ever tried to iron a monster?

Where do monsters live?

On dead-end streets.

How do witches keep their hair in place while flying?

With scare spray.

Why was the witch's broom late?

It over swept.

How do werewolves like their eggs cooked?
Terror-fried.

What did the werewolf say when he ate the monster?
Burp.

What does a vampire use to clean his house?

A victim cleaner.

What is a vampire's favorite holiday?

Fangsgiving.

What's a vampire's favorite candy?

A sucker.

What does a vampire fear the most?

Cavities.

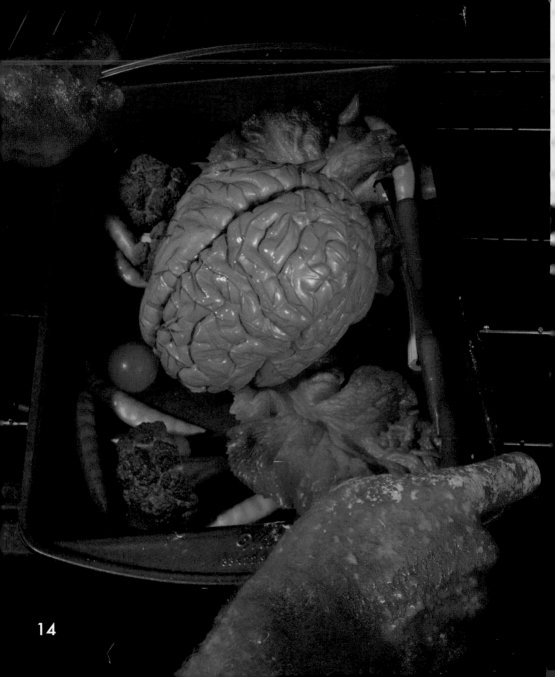

14

What is a zombie's favorite food?

Baked brains.

Who won the zombie soccer game?

No one, it was dead even.

What is a mummy's favorite type of music?

Wrap.

What kind of girl does a mummy take on a date?

Any girl he can dig up!

Skeletons in the Closet

What happens to clumsy ghosts?

They get boo-boos.

Where do young ghosts go during the day?

Dayscare centers.

What does a ghost
eat for lunch?

**A BOO-logna
sandwich.**

When does a ghost
have breakfast?

In the moaning.

Who won the skeleton beauty contest?

No body.

Why didn't the skeleton cross the road?

Because he didn't have the guts.

Read More

Moore, Mark. *Beastly Laughs: A Book of Monster Jokes.* Read-It! Joke Books—Supercharged! Minneapolis: Picture Window Books, 2005.

Rosenberg, Pam. *Monster Jokes.* Laughing Matters. Chanhassen, Minn.: Child's World, 2007.

Schultz, Sam. *Monster Mayhem: Jokes to Scare You Silly.* Make Me Laugh! Minneapolis: Carolrhoda Books, 2004.

Internet Sites

FactHound offers a safe, fun way to find Internet sites related to this book. All of the sites on FactHound have been researched by our staff.

Here's all you do:

Visit *www.facthound.com*

Type in this code: 9781429649988

Word Count: 200   Grade: 1
Early-Intervention Level: 18